MIRACLE MOMENTS IN

SOCCER

KENNY ABDO

Fly!
An Imprint of Abdo Zoom
abdobooks.com

abdobooks.com

Published by Abdo Zoom, a division of ABDO, P.O. Box 398166, Minneapolis, Minnesota 55439. Copyright © 2022 by Abdo Consulting Group, Inc. International copyrights reserved in all countries. No part of this book may be reproduced in any form without written permission from the publisher. Fly!™ is a trademark and logo of Abdo Zoom.

Printed in the United States of America, North Mankato, Minnesota.
052021
092021

Photo Credits: Alamy, AP Images, Getty Images, Granger Collection, Icon Sportswire, iStock, Newscom, Shutterstock
Production Contributors: Kenny Abdo, Jennie Forsberg, Grace Hansen
Design Contributors: Dorothy Toth, Neil Klinepier

Library of Congress Control Number: 2020919500

Publisher's Cataloging-in-Publication Data

Names: Abdo, Kenny, author.
Title: Miracle moments in soccer / by Kenny Abdo
Description: Minneapolis, Minnesota : Abdo Zoom, 2022 | Series: Miracles in sports | Includes online resources and index.
Identifiers: ISBN 9781098223229 (lib. bdg.) | ISBN 9781098223922 (ebook) | ISBN 9781098224271 (Read-to-Me ebook)
Subjects: LCSH: Soccer--History--Juvenile literature. | Soccer--Records--Juvenile literature. | Sports--History--Juvenile literature. | Miracles--Juvenile literature. | Curiosities and wonders--Juvenile literature.
Classification: DDC 796.334--dc23

TABLE OF CONENTS

SOCCER

As the most-watched sport in the world, soccer reigns victorious over every other **pastime**.

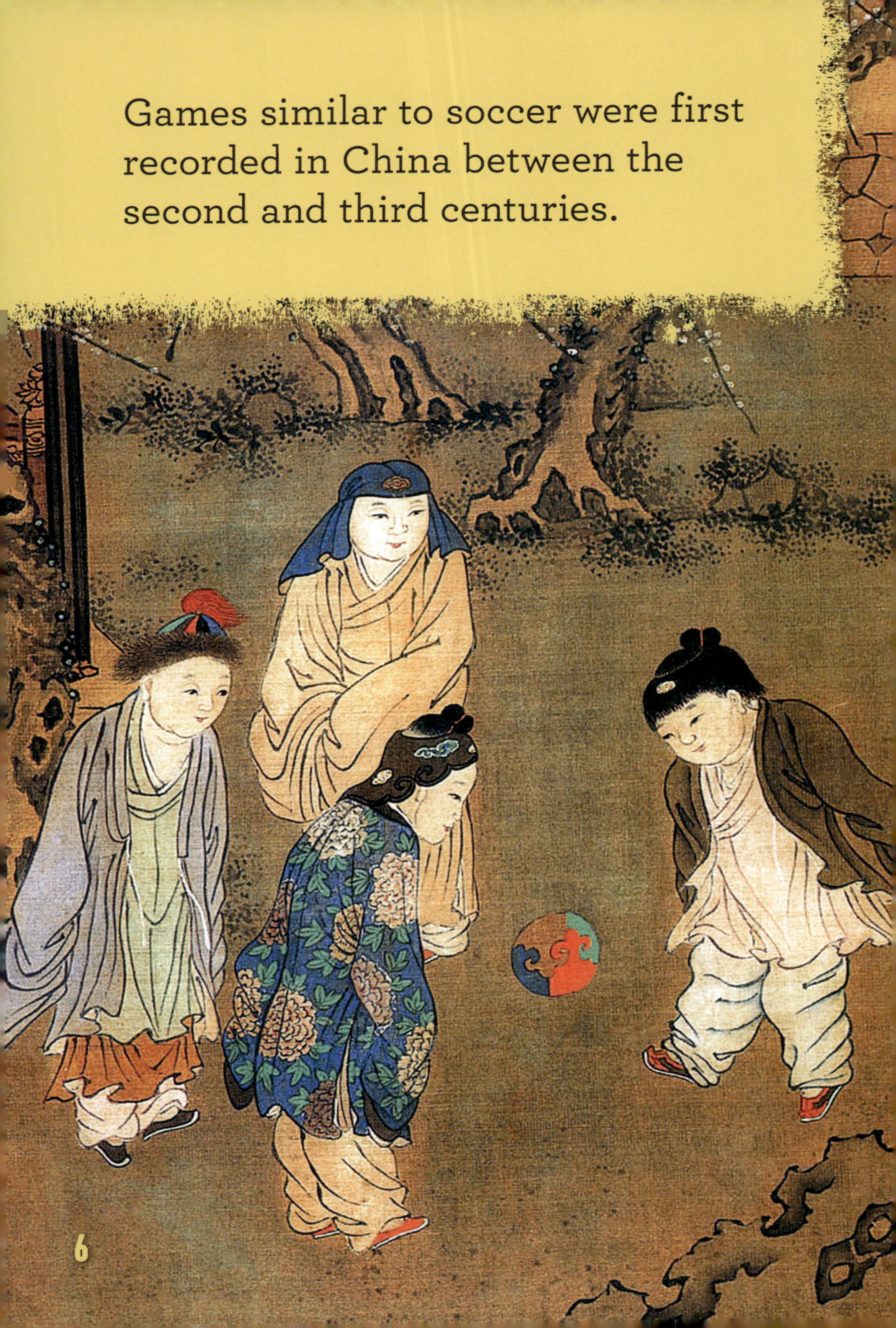

Games similar to soccer were first recorded in China between the second and third centuries.

What we know as soccer today is believed to have started in mid-19th-century England.

Mind-blowing comebacks and wrong-footed victories have all carved themselves into soccer history.

GRIEZMANN
9

DO YOU
BELIEVE?

Antonín Panenka made soccer history during the 1976 European finals. His **chip** won the **Championship** for Czechoslovakia in a **penalty shootout**. Defeating West Germany's harsh goalie, the 'Panenka Penalty' kick was born.

Diego Maradona **scored** the "Goal of the Century" minutes after his infamous "Hand of God" shot. He got the ball and ran 60 yards (55 m) in just 10 seconds to score! Argentina won the game.

Brandi Chastain made the game-winning goal for the USWNT in a **penalty shootout** against China. The 1999 Women's **World Cup** win was witnessed live by more than 90,000 fans and inspired generations to come.

It was not looking good for Liverpool during the 2005 **Champions League**. The team was down 0-3 against Milan. The Reds were able to tie it up within six minutes. Their win is considered one of the greatest comebacks in soccer history.

In 2016, Leicester City did more than break a very long losing streak. They overcame 5,000-to-one betting **odds** by winning the **Premier League**. The team was in last place with nine games to go. They ended up winning seven, **clinching** the **championship**.

LEGACY

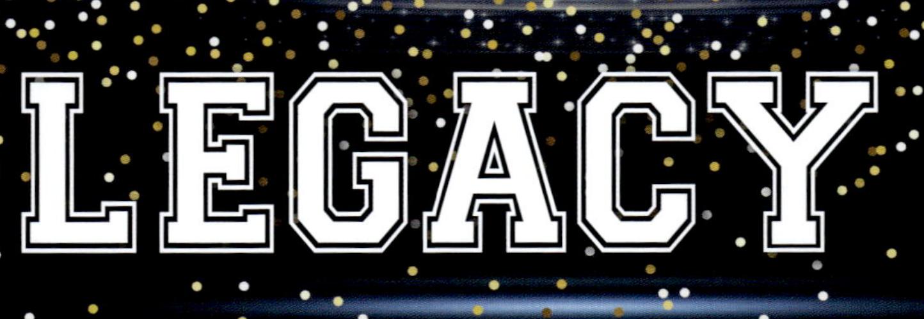

Soccer is so popular that more than 3 billion people tuned in for the 2018 **World Cup**. Miracles on the soccer field have revealed how far teams and players will go to be the best. Which is a goal for everyone!

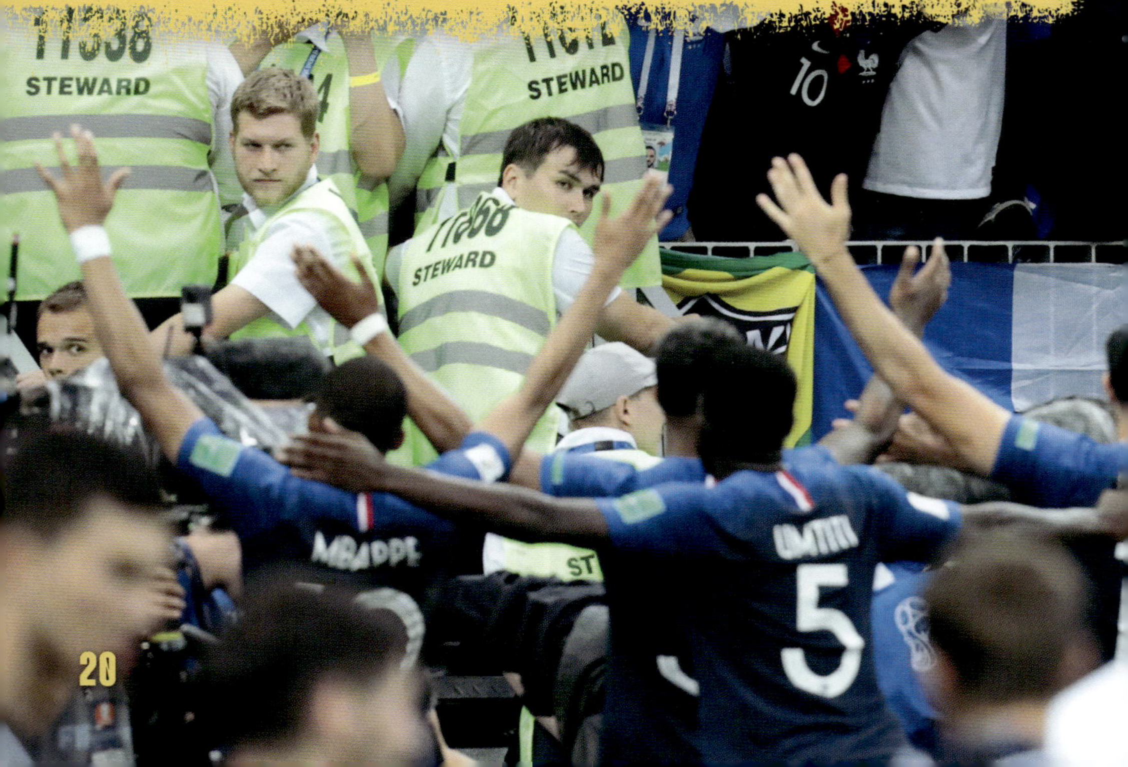

GIROUD
9
TOLISSO
12
LEMAR
8
16

GLOSSARY

Champions League – a yearly club football (soccer) competition organized by the Union of European Football Associations.

championship – a game held to find a first-place winner.

chip – kicking the ball up into the air in a long arc.

clinch – to confirm a win.

odds – the calculated likelihood of a game's outcome.

pastime – an activity people participate in for their enjoyment.

penalty shootout – a method to determine a winner in a soccer match that cannot end in a tie, where 5 players from each team get one kick at the opponent's goal. The team that scores the most goals wins.

Premier League – the top level of the English Football (soccer) league system.

World Cup – an international soccer competition held every four years.

ONLINE RESOURCES

To learn more about miracle moments in soccer, please visit abdobooklinks.com or scan this QR code. These links are routinely monitored and updated to provide the most current information available.

INDEX